WHY THE CAT CHOSE US

John Zeaman

WHY THE CAT CHOSE US

Before They Were Pets

FRANKLIN WATTS
A Division of Grolier Publishing
New York London Hong Kong Sydney
Danbury, Connecticut

Cover and interior design by Robin Hoffman
Illustration p.17 by Karen Kuchar
Illustrations pp. 12, 13, 31, 35, 43 by Stephen Savage

Photographs ©: Animals Animals: 41 (Henry Ausloss), 19 (Esao Hashimoto), 48 (Robert Pearcy); Peter Arnold, Inc.: 39 (James L. Amos); Art Resource: 28 (Bridgeman), 26 (Erich Lessing), 12 (Nimatallah); Alan & Sandy Carey, p. 2; Comstock, 36; Metropolitan Museum of Art, 25; PhotoEdit: 21 (D. Young-Wolff); Photo Researchers, Inc.: 11 (Gregory G. Dimijian), 52 (Jeff Isaac Greenberg), 15 (G. C. Kelly), 51 (Stephen J. Krasemann), 38 (Jean-Michel Labat/Jacana), 36 inset (Carolyn A. McKeone), 16 (Jany Sauvanet), 20 (G. Sommer/Jacana) , 46 (J. P. Varin/Jacana), 33; Stock Montage, Inc.: Charles Walker Collection, 32; Tony Stone Images, Inc: 45 (G. Robert Bishop), 10 (David Epperson), 44 (Renee Lynn), 38 (inset) Don & Pat Valenti; Superstock: 14 (ET Archive, London); Visuals Unlimited: 49 (Walt Anderson), 6 (William J. Weber).

Visit Franklin Watts on the Internet at:
http://publishing.grolier.com

Library of Congress Cataloging-in-Publication Data

Zeaman, John.
Why the cat chose us / John Zeaman.
    p.   cm. (Before they were pets)
Includes bibliographical references and index
Summary: Provides an overview of how wild cats evolved into domesticated cats.
ISBN 0-531-11458-9(lib. bdg.)   0-531-15905-1(pbk.)
1. Cats—Juvenile literature.   2. Wildcat—Juvenile literature. 3. Cats—Behavior—Juvenile literature. 4. Wild cat—Behavior—Juvenile literature. [1. Cats. 2. Wildcat.] I. Title.   II. Series: Zeaman, John. Before they were pets.
SF45.7.Z43 1998
636.8dc21   97-8320
                                                                              CIP
                                                                              AC

CONTENTS

Ordinary house cats, such as this domestic shorthair, still display some of the behaviors of its wild ancestors.

INTRODUCTION

Anyone who has had a pet cat, especially one that goes outside, has probably watched with fascination—and perhaps horror—as the animal stalked a mouse or a bird. First it slinks forward, its body close to the ground. Then it crouches down, staring at the prey, its hind legs making treading motions, its tail twitching in anticipation. Suddenly, it shoots forward, pouncing on its victim.

What's surprising is how close the house cat's behavior is to that of the great predator cats, such as lions and tigers. If you've ever seen a nature film of one of these animals stalking and killing its prey, the actions are amazingly similar. The prey is bigger, but the technique is very much the same.

Here's another unusual thing about cats. Have you ever seen stray cats, the kind that take up residence under a porch, in a basement, or in a barn? You may feel sorry for these cats because they have no one to take care of them, and, in fact, their lives may be difficult. But many cats live this way, perhaps getting scraps from humans or scavenging from garbage cans. Barn cats, who feed on rodents, live entirely by hunting.

These cats have lives that are very close to those of wild animals. In fact, cats are quite capable of living entirely on their own. Such animals, if they haven't had much contact with people, will run and hide when a person approaches, just like any wild animal.

As pets, then, cats are unusual. They were the last of the domesticated animals to be tamed—perhaps only 5,000 years ago—and their independent ways may be an indication that cats are not yet as completely tamed as dogs or cattle. So, just what kind of an animal is our cat? How can the same animal be an affectionate pet one moment, sitting on our lap and purring contentedly, and be a ruthless hunter the next? And what if our beloved pet was as big as a lion or a tiger, would it decide to hunt us as well?

CHAPTER 1
TAME OR WILD?

The earliest evidence of cat **domestication** is an Egyptian tomb painting from 2600 B.C. that shows a cat wearing a collar. Even stronger evidence comes from a tomb dating to 1900 B.C. in which the bones of 17 cats were found along with little pots of offerings of milk.

From 1600 B.C. on, the evidence of cats as pets is abundant. Many tomb paintings show cats sitting under chairs, and others show them eating fish, gnawing on bones, and playing with other animals. In one painting, a cat is tied to a chair leg with a ribbon.

Scientists, however, believe that cat domestication happened much earlier than 2600 B.C. Cat bones have

A tortoise-shell shorthair cat sneaks through high grass in search of prey. Although cats have been tamed, they still display some of the behaviors of their wild ancestors.

been found among the bones and other debris left by ancient cave-dwelling people. Scientists cannot be sure if these bones belonged to tame cats or not. These cats may simply have been eaten, just as other wild animals were.

One of the problems scientists have in pinning down the time that cats began to live with people is that cats have not evolved or changed much in the shift from wild to tame. The skeletons of wild cats are often identical to the skeletons of domesticated ones.

CATS AS HUNTERS

Cats are very good at catching mice and seem particularly interested in animals that disappear into holes. They are less skillful at catching birds, although some can do it well. That's because birds escape by flying up, and a cat's body is designed to pounce down. It loses its balance if it tries to pursue something above it. Some cats will kill rats, but a rat is a formidable opponent for a cat and, if cornered, will leap at a cat's face. A cat who learns to kill rats often employs a different technique: it braces itself with its hind legs, pulls its head back, and swats at the rat with its paws, knocking it senseless.

A domestic cat stalks a rock dove. Cats are very good hunters, but they're much better at catching mice and other rodents than birds.

REMAINING WILD

Why have cats changed so little physically, when other domesticated animals, such as dogs—which evolved from wolves—have changed so much? Perhaps this is because cats continue to be hunters, even after they are tamed. They are also very independent in raising their kittens, teaching their young to fend for themselves the same way their wild counterparts do. Other domesticated animals have lost this ability.

But this only raises another question. Why have cats continued to act this way after becoming pets? All the other domesticated animals have given up their wild ways. A dog may sometimes kill a squirrel or even another dog, but dogs are no longer the efficient predators that their ancestors the wolves are.

The answer lies in the way cats became domesticated. Unlike other domesticated animals, cats were not captured and tamed and bred to live with people. They began by living very close to human communities. They crept in closer and closer to human settlements because they were attracted by rodents. In killing the rodents, cats proved their value to people. So the cat's hunting ability—an essential part of its wild character—was something that people liked and didn't want to change.

Eventually, the cat moved right into the human house. We may think of the cat as a pet, but the cat, if it could think like a person, certainly wouldn't see itself as a pet. From the cat's point of view, it chose to live with people because it found an easier, better life.

CHAPTER 2

DOMESTICATION OF THE CAT

The ordinary domestic cat has changed very little in appearance and behavior from its ancestor, the African wild cat, also called the Egyptian cat or the Kaffir cat. This cat, which scientists call *Felis silvestris lybica*, has existed for about a million years. Despite its name, it is found in many places besides Africa, including a number of Mediterranean islands, the Middle East, Arabia, India, and Turkestan.

The African wild cat is larger than the average domestic cat—36 inches (91 cm) from nose to tail tip—and it has longer legs, a leaner body, and a long, thin tail. The backs of its ears are a bright rust

This ancient Egyptian tomb painting shows a cat crouching under a chair. Scientists believe that Egyptians were the first people to tame cats.

An African wild cat roams the Kalahari Desert in South Africa. Scientists believe that this type of cat is the main ancestor of the domestic cat.

color. It can be almost any solid color, or there may be thin broken stripes on its body. The African wild cat's eyes are rimmed with black lines, like eye makeup. It's thought that Egyptian ladies got the idea for lining their own eyes from observing their beloved cats.

A slightly different form of this animal is the European wild cat, or *Felis silvestris silvestris*. Because it lives in a colder climate, this cat is stockier than the African one and has thicker fur. Some scientists have theorized that our domestic cats may have descended from the European

A European wild cat climbs a tree in eastern France. Although this cat looks like an ordinary tabby, it cannot be tamed.

wild cat because its striped fur pattern occurs in the most common kind of modern cat—the type we call tabbies, or tigers. But, appearance isn't everything. Despite its resemblance to domestic cats, the European wild cat is quite untamable. Even if people raise it from kittenhood, it remains fierce and nasty.

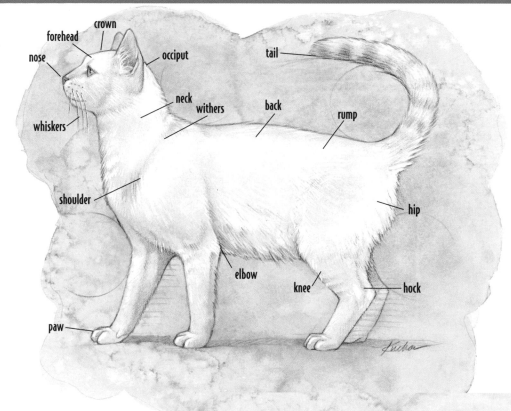

CAT ANATOMY

Cats have the same basic skeletons as humans. They have rounded heads and short muzzles, or snouts. Cats are muscular and well coordinated, and their bodies are very flexible.

Sprinters

Cats can run very fast for very short distances. When a cat runs, its limbs are totally extended in the air. When its forefeet hit the ground, its flexible spine bends like a spring, allowing the rear end to continue moving forward in a fluid motion. A cat can reach a speed of about 31 miles (50 kilometers) per hour, but only for a few moments.

The African wild cat, in contrast, often approaches human settlements in search of rodents. Even today, these wild cats are frequently tamed by people. And because the first house cats were found in Egypt, scientists believe the African wild cat is the main ancestor of our pets, and that the European wild cat was crossbred with these later, contributing its striped coat.

MOVING IN

Some scientists set the date of cat domestication at 7000 B.C. in the ancient city of Jericho. It may very well have happened earlier, but this is the first strong evidence of cats living side by side with people. So many cat bones have been found in Jericho that it's reasonable to suppose that some of these cats must have been tamed. Even if the cats were only scavengers or were used for food, the natural human impulse to tame would have meant that a few cats probably became pets.

One bit of interesting evidence of cat domestication comes from the Mediterranean island of Cyprus. A feline jawbone was found there that dates to the year 6000 B.C. Why is it so unusual? It is because the island of Cyprus has no wild cats. **Archaeologists** believe that the cat must have been brought to the island by early human settlers. Since they would not have taken a wild cat with them on a difficult sea voyage, scientists assume the cat was already domesticated by that time.

How exactly did cats find their way into human communities? There is no way to know for sure, because there is no history written during this ancient period. But scientists can theorize about what may have happened, based on their knowledge of ancient civilizations and their observations of cat behavior.

They believe that cats probably weren't tamed until people began to farm. This happened during the Neolithic period (from about 8000 B.C. to 3000 B.C.), which is also called the New Stone Age. In the Old Stone Age, people were nomadic hunter-gatherers. They didn't live in a fixed place. They tamed the wolf because it was useful for protection and as a hunting companion. But people at this time had no use for cats.

On the other hand, farming requires that people stay in one place. So once people discovered how to grow their own food, most of them gave up their nomadic way of life, settled down, and built permanent shelters. Farming also

A stray cat investigates a garbage can in an alley. Some cats still live at the fringe of human settlements, much as their ancestors did.

WHY DO CATS PLAY WITH THEIR PREY?

When a cat catches something, it often seems to play with its victim, repeatedly letting it go and recapturing it, as if for sport. This kind of behavior is one reason some people think of cats as cruel. Scientists think this is because cats build up excess energy prior to a hunt. If the capture is too easy, however, a cat still has excess energy that it needs to spend. This is also why a house cat will sometimes get up and dash madly around the house for no apparent reason. People used to think this meant the cat was possessed by the devil. However, it has built up excess energy that it has to use up to feel comfortable again.

A black cat devours a field mouse. Cats will sometimes play with their prey, and scientists think they do it to expend excess energy.

produces more food than can be eaten at one time, so early farmers had to find places to store their crops as grain.

The farmers' storehouses of grain would have immediately attracted rats and mice. These rodents would have quickly infested the storehouses, not only consuming large amounts of grain but also fouling it with their droppings. Nowadays, with modern storage facilities and extermination methods, we don't realize what a serious problem rodents can be. But for these ancient people, living in a warm climate, the rapidly multiplying rodents must have seemed like a kind of plague.

Any animal that preyed on these rats and mice would have seemed like a gift from the gods. Imagine their surprise when they began to notice that cats, acting entirely on their own, were doing a job that no human could do as well. For the cats, the situation must have seemed too good to believe. Instead of having to stalk solitary mice in the thick underbrush, they would have found an abundance of well-fed mice right there for the taking.

A NEW WAY OF LIFE

Clearly, cats and people found a mutually beneficial relationship. By this time, humans had already domesticated many animals, so the idea of keeping and breeding useful creatures was not new. People would have immediately begun to tame and raise their own cats. In a short time, cats graduated from guarding the storehouses to keeping human houses free of rodents, too.

Its important to understand, however, that in moving into the human house and sharing space with people, the cat had to make a fundamental change in its behavior. Of all the members of the cat family, only lions live in social

A cat enjoys the attention of two friends. Wild cats are not social animals, so when they moved in with humans, their behavior changed.

groups. Dogs adapted easily to life with people because they, too, are social animals and see people as part of their pack. But cats are not social. They live entirely on their own and will fight with other cats that invade their territory.

So, how did such an independent animal become a social creature?

The answer lies in the process of domestication. When animals become domesticated, they tend to retain more juvenile behaviors. That's why domesticated animals are usually more playful than wild animals. Although a cat is solitary, there are times in its life when it does live in a group: when it is part of a litter or is being mother to a litter. Hence, scientists think that some genetic change as a result of being domesticated makes cats stay in a kittenish phase for their entire adult lives. According to this view, cats see their owners as mother cats. And, as we will see, many of their behaviors toward people certainly suggest that this is true.

How Does a Cat Find Its Way Home?

Scientific tests have shown that cats can find their way home even after being driven several miles and dropped in a strange place. Scientists believe cats have a built-in homing mechanism that is tied to a sensitivity to the Earth's magnetic field.

CHAPTER 3

CAT LOVERS AND CAT HATERS

Imagine a society in which the people worshiped catlike gods, and cats were so respected that they were considered sacred. That was the situation in ancient Egypt. The Egyptians valued cats so much that killing one was punishable by death.

The relationship between Egyptians and cats began in a practical way. Cats were kept in large numbers to guard the huge communal storehouses of grain, or granaries, along the banks of the Nile River. Cats also guarded the granaries of individual homeowners. Soon the cat's hunting abilities were put to other uses. They were encouraged to

patrol gardens, where they would kill or scare away venomous snakes. Later, they even became retrievers, fetching downed wildfowl in the marshes for their hunter masters.

One of the Egyptian goddesses, Bastet, is depicted as a woman with a cat's head. She was said to have a special relationship with cats and could come to Earth whenever she wished and take the form of a cat. That was one of the reasons no one could kill or hurt a cat. The Egyptians had special cat holidays. In the temple of Bastet, at the city of Bubastis, cats slept on soft cushions in the shrine, ate the choicest foods, and were lovingly attended by the priests.

This Egyptian painting shows two cats relaxing with a family. Egyptians held cats in high regard, and killing a cat was outlawed.

This bronze statue depicts the Egyptian goddess Bastet, who sometimes took the form of a cat.

GUARDING
THEIR TERRITORY

Cats are not social animals. Except when they are raising a family, they hunt and live alone. In the wild, each cat has its own personal resting or sleeping place that it will defend from other cats and a home range, which it patrols but may share with other cats. Cats mark their territory with a foul-smelling spray so other cats will know that it is theirs. In the wild, this preserves a balance of nature. If too many cats hunt in the same place, there will not be enough food for them all. But house cats who are fed at home don't realize that this behavior serves no purpose in human neighborhoods, and they will zealously guard their backyard from all invaders.

Each Egyptian family had a cat, which they treated with tender care. The house cats of rich Egyptians wore gold rings in their ears, and servants took care of them. When a pet cat died, the family members went into mourning, shaving off their eyebrows as a sign of deep respect. They held an elaborate funeral during which they drank wine and beat their breasts in sorrow. The dead cat was carefully embalmed, wrapped in strips of linen cloth, and its face was covered with a sculptured wooden mask. The cat was then enclosed in the most expensive mummy case the family could afford, sometimes in the shape of a cat. The tiny **mummy** was placed in the family tomb or

Cat mummies, such as this one, have been found in the tombs of ancient Egyptians.

buried in a cat cemetery, often with tiny mummies of mice, shrews, and other food for the cat to eat in the afterworld.

In 1888, more than 300,000 mummified cats were found in an Egyptian cemetery. Sadly, the cat mummies were stripped of their wrappings and carted off to be used by farmers in England and the United States for fertilizer!

From pictures, the sacred cats of Egypt appear to resemble today's Siamese and Abyssinian breeds, so it is very likely that the Egyptians had already begun to breed cats for particular looks.

SPREADING ACROSS THE WORLD

Cats were so sacred in Egypt that the Egyptians didn't want anyone else to have them. Smuggling a cat out of the country was forbidden, and the law was enforced with the death penalty. For about a thousand years, the Egyptians were successful in preventing the export of their sacred cats. But Phoenician sailors, notorious for their shady dealings, were determined to get their hands on these valuable animals. Eventually, they succeeded in smuggling the useful felines out of Egypt and selling them to rich people in Athens, Rome, and other important cities around the Mediterranean. From there, cats spread across Europe as the Roman Empire expanded.

For centuries, cats continued to be appreciated by people. A tenth-century law in Wales shows how much cats were valued. If someone killed a cat, the person had to pay a fine in grain. The amount of grain was determined by hanging the corpse of the cat by the tail with the nose touching the ground. The cat killer was then made to heap up as much of his own grain as it would take to cover the

Cat Litters

Most cats give birth to between one and nine kittens. The largest litter ever produced was 19 kittens, 15 of which survived.

This sculpture depicts three Greeks with a cat and a dog. Sailors smuggled cats out of Egypt and sold them to people in other countries, including Greece.

cat. The pile was supposed to represent how much grain the cat would have saved from mice if it hadn't been killed.

BEWITCHED

In the Middle Ages, however, the fortunes of the cat began to decline. As cats multiplied, their value in people's eyes decreased. The Christian church identified the cat with pagan religions. Not only did the Egyptians have a cat god, but in Roman mythology, the moon goddess, Diana, was thought to take the form of a cat. And Diana had a double identity: she sometimes became Hecate, a goddess of witchcraft and the underworld.

As the Christian church spread in power and influence, it tried to stamp out the pagan religions. Cats began to be seen as sly, evil creatures—the companions of witches. People in the Middle Ages were very superstitious. They believed that witches were agents of the devil and that cats could be witches' familiars, or helpers, and aid them in their evil work. People even believed that the witches themselves took the shape of cats to roam the night undetected. Many of the people accused of being witches were eccentric old women who kept many cats for company. These people were often tortured and made to confess to all kinds of impossible crimes. Often they were executed, along with their cats.

As the witch hysteria spread, so did the hatred and distrust of cats. Cruelty to cats was encouraged as a way of triumphing over evil. On St. John's Day, people all over Europe stuffed cats into sacks and tossed them into bonfires. On holy days, people celebrated by tossing cats from a church tower. Cats were tied together by the tail and people watched while the frightened animals bit and clawed at each other to get free.

Medieval Europeans paid a heavy price for their persecution of cats. Rats began to overrun European cities, and the fleas that they spread carried a terrible new disease: **bubonic plague**. In the 14th century, this plague killed about 25 million people in just two years. Those who owned cats, which kept their houses and farms free of rats, fared better than their cat-hating neighbors. Gradually, the value of cats was realized again.

Do Cats Have a Sixth Sense?

Cats are extremely sensitive to vibrations, and there are many reports of cats acting strangely prior to earthquakes. Apparently, cats are able to detect the first tremors 10 or 15 minutes before humans can.

This 16th-century illustration shows a witch with her black cat. Cats became objects of scorn in the Middle Ages because they were thought to be witches' helpers.

In this 17th-century illustration, doctors at a German plague hospital try to heal their patients. The bubonic plague swept through Europe in the 1300s, and there were periodic outbreaks of the disease for centuries.

Some remnants of the superstitions about cats still persist from the Middle Ages, however. Many people still think that a black cat crossing their path brings bad luck. Others believe that cats can suck the breath from a sleeping baby.

CHAPTER 4

BREEDS OF CATS

Although most of the 500 million cats in the world today are mixed-breed cats, many people favor an animal with an unusual and attractive appearance. For this reason, cat fanciers have bred a variety of purebred cats with different types of fur, unusual colors, and different-shaped faces and bodies. Today, there are about 26 breeds of cats, divided into three broad groups: **domestic shorthairs**, **foreign** or **oriental shorthairs**, and **longhairs**.

DOMESTIC SHORTHAIRS

The domestic shorthair is the most common of the breeds. These cats come in a number of colors and markings. The tiger, or tabby, is marked by dark striping on the head, back, sides, and legs. Tabby cats typically come in shades of black and gray or orange. The mackerel tabby has narrow vertical stripes marking the sides of its body from shoulder to tail, and it is thought to be closer to the original wild cats. The black lines on the tabby cats forehead form an almost perfect M, and unbroken lines running down its cheeks from the outer corner of each eye make it look as though it is wearing eye makeup.

Tortoiseshell and calico cats have multicolored coats. A tortoiseshell cat is basically black, with patches of orange and cream. A calico cat is a white cat, with patches of orange and black, and white underparts. Both types are nearly always females. The reason for this has to do with the genes for fur color. **Genes** are tiny units in each cell that determine which qualities a living creature will get from its parents. In cats, the genes for orange and black fur are linked to the genes that make cats female rather than male. So male cats can't get both an orange and a black gene. They can be solid orange or solid black, but not both, unless they have an abnormal number of genes.

Another shorthair variation is the pure white cat. Many animal species occasionally have offspring that are pure white because they lack the genes for making the dark pigment **melanin**, which gives color to hair, eyes, and skin. These white animals, called **albinos**, have pink eyes, reflecting the color of the blood flowing in tiny blood vessels at the back of the eyes. But

Why Do Cats Groom Themselves?

Not just to keep themselves clean. Cats lick their fur to smooth it so that it will be a better insulator in cold weather. By licking the fur and making it wet, the cat can cool itself off in hot weather.

This typical household cat is an example of a domestic shorthair.

Pure white cats are albinos, which means that they lack a gene for making the dark pigment that gives color to the eyes. This white cat has blue eyes, which means that it's probably deaf.

most white cats are not true albinos. They have blue eyes. Unfortunately, most blue-eyed white cats are also deaf. Breeders who have tried to breed out the deafness by crossing blue-eyed white cats with other varieties came up with a curious result: odd-eyed white cats with one blue eye and one orange eye.

FOREIGN SHORTHAIRS

Siamese cats are believed to be descended from ancient Egyptian cats but were developed into a unique breed in 17th-century Thailand. They have a slender build and a triangular head, with bright blue eyes slightly slanted toward the nose. Siamese kittens are born white, but as they grow, the head, legs, and tail gradually darken. The dark areas are called points. In 1930, two Russian biologists discovered that the color change in Siamese kittens depends on their body temperature. Siamese cats carry albino genes of a special kind that work only when the body temperature is above 98°F (37°C). If these kittens are kept in a very warm room, their points will not darken, and they will remain a creamy white.

LONGHAIRS

The Persian cat originated in 16th-century Iran and may have been bred from the native Asian Steppe cat rather than the African wild cat. The Persian's long, thick fur, stocky build, and small ears seem to indicate that it came from a cold region.

   The Himalayan and Balinese cats are long-haired cats with the markings of a Siamese. The Himalayan was bred by mating Persian and Siamese cats. The Balinese origi-

Cat Shows

The first cat show took place in London in 1871. Shows, which usually last two days, are sponsored by such clubs as the Cat Fanciers Association (CFA) or the International Cat Association (TICA). Cats are judged according to their color and breed. Even an ordinary house cat can enter many cat shows. The cat who wins the most ribbons will be judged the overall champion.

37

Himalayans, such as this kitten, are long-haired cats that have the markings of a Siamese.

Persians are a type of longhair. This Persian Blue-point has the long, thick fur, stocky build, and small ears of the Persian type.

nated in a different way. Occasionally, two Siamese cats will produce a long-haired offspring. By breeding these rare long-haired cats together, breeders eventually created a new breed of long-haired Siamese.

UNUSUAL BREEDS

The tailless Manx cat, from the Isle of Man, is about 400 years old and comes in two varieties: the more common

It's easy to recognize a Manx cat because it has no tail.

Big Cats, Little Cats

Most adult cats weigh from 6 pounds (2 kg) to 12 pounds (5 kg). The heaviest cat on record weighed 42 pounds (14 kg). The lightest adult cat weighed 1 pound, 12 ounces (0.8 kg).

stumpies, which have just a short stump of a tail, and the rumpies, which are completely tailless and are the only ones shown in cat shows. The Manx's hind legs are so long that the animals seem to hop when they run.

There are many legends about the Manx. According to one, it lost its tail because it was the last animal to board Noah's ark. With the great flood rising fast, Noah slammed the door of the ark in such a hurry that he accidentally cut off the cat's fine bushy tail. Another legend says that the animal's hopping gait is the result of mating between a rabbit and a cat.

Another cat with a legendary origin is the Maine Coon cat. New Englanders claim it is the result of a cross between a raccoon and a cat. They are large cats: Males often weigh 40 pounds (18 kg), and females more than 20 pounds (9 kg). This breed has a heavy, muscular build with broad "snowshoe" feet that permit it to move easily across the winter snow.

Animal breeders are always striving to create new breeds. The Scottish Fold, for example, is the only cat that has floppy ears. The Canadian Sphynx is a hairless cat first discovered in Ontario in 1966. It is valued by people who are allergic to cats. Its lack of fur, however, makes it unappealing to many cat enthusiasts and leaves it vulnerable to the cold.

The most unusual breed is the Ragdoll, which has an unusually limp body. When picked up, it simply hangs in your hands like a ragdoll. The American Peke-face cat is a long-haired cat that has been bred for a flat face, giving it a rounded, babylike appearance that makes it appealing to humans.

Cats bred for very unusual appearances or behaviors may have serious health problems. The limp-bodied Rag-

The Canadian Sphynx has no hair.

doll, for example, is more likely to be injured in accidents or by people dropping it. Burmese cats, as a result of breeding for extremely short faces, may be born with cleft skulls. Siamese cats are more likely than other cats to have heart defects.

CHAPTER 5 CAT BEHAVIOR

Stuck in a Tree

Cats are good climbers, but they are no great shakes at getting down. Their claws are curved the wrong way for going backwards and their legs can't spread like a squirrel's. To get down, they must slither down awkwardly.

Today, cats are one of the most popular pets in the world, and people seem endlessly fascinated by their behavior and their unusual abilities. Some of these qualities are highlighted in expressions or sayings about cats.

We say "curiosity killed the cat" because cats have a way of getting into trouble sometimes, often getting trapped in places they can't get out of. But when cats do survive such ordeals, we say the cat has "nine lives." That's because cats can live for long periods of time without food or water. Many stories are told of cats being accidentally locked in garages, or even in crates, then emerging weeks, even months later. Some have survived trips under the hoods of cars and others have endured journeys in the unpressurized cargo hold of a jetliner.

The cat's reputation for having nine lives also comes from its ability to survive falls from great heights by turning its body in space so that it lands on its feet. But even without nine lives, cats are the longest-lived of all the small domestic animals: 13 to 15 years for males, 15 to 17 years for females. **Neutered** animals live an average of one to two years longer. But strays that forage on their own live only six to eight years, by which time their teeth may be worn down to the gums. So, one of the advantages of pethood for cats is a doubled life span. That's quite a benefit.

THE MYSTERY OF CATS

Cats can seem like mysterious creatures, even to people who own them. For example, they often seem to be staring out into space rather than looking at anything in particular. People find this eerie, but the reason for it is that cats do not see the same way we do. Their vision is not as sharp they don't focus as well as we do, but they are very good at picking up motion, which helps them hunt.

Cats' eyes also look different from our eyes because they have oval-shaped pupils. Cats also have a mirror-like layer inside the eye called the **tapetum**, which helps collect more light. This is why a cat's eyes shine in the dark, a feature that has fascinated people for centuries.

Have you ever noticed that a cat doesn't like to have its whiskers touched? Whiskers are organs of touch that scientists call vibrissae, and they are supersensitive. They are so sensitive that they help a cat find its way in total darkness by picking up tiny wind currents that tell them

Seeing in the Dark

Cats have excellent night vision. One reason is that their eyes are very large for their size. Also, the cats retina—the light-sensitive part of the eye—has many cells that are active in dim light. The tapetum reflects more light within the eye. Contrary to popular belief, however, cats cannot see in total darkness.

43

Cats' eyes are very different than humans' eyes. Cats can see well in the dark and are good at picking up motion, which helps them in hunting.

Can Cats See Colors?

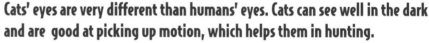

Yes, but rather poorly. People used to think that cats were color-blind, but tests have shown that they can see most colors. However, cats are much more sensitive to the degree of grayness of colors than to the colors themselves. That's because their eyes are much better at seeing in dim light.

where objects are in a room. Because the whiskers stick out so far from the face, they can also help a cat judge whether a space is wide enough for it to crawl into.

Cats can smell better than we can, although they cannot smell as well as a dog. But did you know that a cat can smell certain odors through its mouth? Cats have a scent organ in the roof of their mouth called the **Jacobsons organ**, which picks up odors emitted by other cats. When a cat senses odors with its Jacobson's organ, it makes a curious grimace with its mouth open. This is called flehmen.

A cat's whiskers are very sensitive and can help a cat find its way in the dark.

45

TWISTING IN SPACE

There's an old saying that a falling cat will always land on its feet, and this is often true. Cats have balance organs in their ears that help them turn themselves in space during a fall, and their flexible spine allows them to quickly get in the right position. Strangely, a cat can more easily survive a fall from a ten-story window than from a three-story window. Why? After falling about three stories, a cat reaches maximum falling speed and is able to relax and spread out its legs to slow itself down like a parachutist. Relaxed limbs are less likely to break on impact with the ground.

This time-lapse photograph shows how a cat lands when dropped. Cats can even turn themselves in space during a fall.

A cat's nose has another interesting function: it can sense temperature. That is why a cat may suddenly back away from hot food after approaching with its nose. It's the temperature, not the smell, that causes the reaction.

Perhaps a cat's nose is especially sensitive because the rest of its body is not. For example, cats can walk on snow or ice without any apparent discomfort. They are less sensitive to heat, too. That's why cats will snuggle up to radiators too hot for humans to touch.

BALANCING ACT

Have you ever noticed that a cat can walk comfortably on a tree branch or a very narrow ledge? One reason it can do this is that it has a long, flexible tail that it uses to keep its balance. The other reason is that a cat's leg joints swing and rotate much more freely than ours do. When a cat walks, its front feet swing out and in so that the feet line up one in front of the other. As a result, a cat can walk comfortably on a ledge only 2 inches (5 cm) wide.

TOOTH AND NAIL

A cat has very sharp claws. The reason they stay sharp is that they are retractable. A cat can pull its claws back into protective sheaths, so the claws are not dulled by walking. When they do need to be sharpened, a cat scratches its claws against a tree, or on a chair, which scrapes off the claw's outer layer, exposing a fresh point.

Have you ever seen a cat yawn and noticed what frightening teeth it has? A cat's teeth are made for cutting and tearing the flesh of its prey. The most impressive teeth are the four long canines, or fangs. These teeth are minia-

How Do Cats Retract Their Claws?

Each of a cat's claws is attached to a bone in the toe. By flexing its toe (just as we bend our fingers), a cat can retract the claw into the foot. When a cat points its toe, the claw is extended.

47

A cat shows its sharp claws while playing with string. The claws stay sharp because a cat can pull its claws back into protective sheaths.

This cat's yawn reveals its impressive teeth. A cat's teeth are very much like those of lions and tigers.

ture versions of the ones lions and tigers have, and are used for the killing bite. When a cat kills its prey, it goes for the back of its neck, pushing these long, sharp teeth between the prey's vertebrae and severing the spinal cord.

WHY DO CATS SLEEP SO MUCH?

Cats sleep twice as much as we do, about 16 hours out of every 24. That means that a nine-year-old cat has only been awake for a total of about three years. Very few mammals sleep this much. The reason a cat can spend so much time sleeping is because it is such an efficient hunter. It doesn't have to spend a lot of time searching and chasing its game. It sits and waits, stalks a little, then kills its prey. Cats don't sleep for a long stretch of time. They take lots of short naps during the day and the night. That's why we call a short nap a catnap.

COMMUNICATION

Cats communicate in two ways: either vocally or with body language.

Purring is a sound unique to cats. Most owners enjoy having a purring cat on their lap. Why do cats purr? Kittens first purr when they are nursing from their mother. Their purring tells the mother that the milk is getting to the kittens, and she, in turn, purrs to them, letting them know that all is well. So when a cat purrs it generally means it's contented, although some cats will purr when they are hurt or need help.

A cat shows anger by narrowing its eyes and putting its ears back. A cat that's ready to fight stands tall and raises the fur on its back. But a frightened cat crouches low, with its fur raised all over its body, making it look bigger than it is.

This cat stands tall and raises the fur on its back to show that it is ready to fight.

KITTENISH BEHAVIOR

Because domesticated cats are more kittenish, they relate to us as if we were their mother. And this is what makes domestic cats social animals.

One way that pet cats act like kittens is that they let us stroke them. A mother cat grooms her kittens by licking them. When we stroke a cat, it is experiencing something similar. That's why a cat will follow after us, gazing

51

Why Do Cats Purr?

Young cats purr when nursing to tell the mother that they are content. A mother cat purrs when she approaches her litter to tell them, "It's me, not an enemy." Older kittens purr when they try to get adult cats to play. Sick cats purr at the approach of another cat to say, "Leave me be, I'm not a threat to you."

A girl caresses her cat. Pet cats often act like kittens, letting people stroke them.

with affection at us and inviting us to pet it. Our hand is like a giant tongue to the cat.

Another kittenish behavior is the way a cat will press its paws into our laps, as if it were trampling or kneading something. This behavior goes back to the time when the cat was nursing from its mother. Kittens press their paws up against her in just this way to make the milk flow.

Even the way a cat greets us is kittenish. It approaches with a soft, birdlike chirp, its tail elevated and held vertically, sometimes with the end curled over into a question mark. It usually rubs itself against our hand or legs, purring loudly and, occasionally, rolling around on its back. These same signals generally occur in greetings between kittens and their mother.

It is interesting to observe how the qualities that make cats valuable to people have changed. People first welcomed cats into their homes because cats could kill mice. After cats were domesticated, they became different animals. They continued to hunt mice, but they became more social, more playful, and more affectionate creatures. They became pets. There are still many people in the world who depend on cats for their mouse-killing abilities. But many, many others enjoy them purely as companions. Either way, cats have found a permanent home in the human community.

Expressive Ears

Cats show expression with their ears. If a cat's ears are pointed forward they convey friendly interest and attentiveness. Ears pricked up and turned slightly backward are a warning that attack is imminent. Ears bent back and drawn down sideways show fear and readiness to take flight.

GLOSSARY

albino A person or animal whose skin, hair and eyes lack normal pigment. The skin and body hair is white, and the eyes appear pink.

archaeologists Scientists who study the way humans and animals lived a very long time ago. They dig up the remains of ancient cities or settlements and study bones, weapons, pottery, and other things they find. They also dig up the remains of domestic animals and study their bones to learn how they lived and changed over time.

bubonic plague A highly contagious disease that causes large lumps, or bubos, to appear in the armpit or groin. It also causes fever, exhaustion, and delirium. Fleas from infected rats are the carriers.

55

domestication   The act of training or changing a wild animal so that it can benefit people.

domestic shorthairs   The most common type of cat. The two main types are the British Shorthair and the American Shorthair. They have sturdy bodies and rounded heads.

foreign shorthairs   A group of cats that have wedge-shaped heads with slanting eyes and large pointed ears. They have slim bodies, long legs, and a very fine short coat. Also called Oriental shorthairs.

genes   The tiny units of a cell of an animal or plant that determine the characteristics that an offspring inherits from its parent or parents.

Jacobson's organ   A second organ of smell that cats and some other animals have. It is located on the roof of the mouth.

longhairs   A group of cats with long coats bred in Asia beginning in the late 1500s. Most longhairs are of the breed known as Persian. They have a sturdy, rounded body, short legs, and a round face with a short nose and large, round eyes. Their luxurious coats can be as long as 5 inches (12 cm).

melanin   A brownish-black pigment found in skin, hair, and other animal tissues.

mummy   A dead body of person or an animal that has been wrapped in cloth and preserved. Many mummies are found in ancient Egyptian tombs.

neutered   An animal that has had its sex organs altered or removed by surgery so that it cannot reproduce.

tapetum   A reflective membrane located inside the eye of cats and some other nocturnal animals that helps to gather light within the eye.

FOR FURTHER INFORMATION

BOOKS

Alderton, David. *Cats*. New York: Dorling Kindersley, 1992.

Clutton-Brock, Juliet. *Cat*. New York: Knopf, 1991.

Overbeck, Cynthia. *Cats*. Minneapolis: Lerner, 1983.

Silverstein, Alvin and Virginia. *Cats: All About Them*. New York: Lothrop, Lee & Shepard, 1978.

Trumble, Kelly. *Cat Mummies*. New York: Clarion, 1996.

FOR ADVANCED READERS

Beadle, Muriel. *The Cat: History, Biology, and Behavior*. New York: Simon & Schuster, 1977.

Caras, Roger. *A Cat is Watching*. New York: Simon & Schuster, 1989.

Clutton-Brock, Juliet. *A Natural History of Domesticated Animals*. Austin: University of Texas Press, 1989.

Hazen, Barbara Shook. *The Dell Encyclopedia of Cats*. New York: Delacorte Press, 1974.

Milani, Myrna M. *The Body Language and Emotion of Cats*. New York: William Morrow, 1987.

Morris, Desmond. *Catwatching*. New York: Crown, 1986. *Catlore*. New York: Crown, 1987.

Taylor, David. *The Ultimate Cat Book*. Simon & Schuster, 1989.

Wratten, Peggy. *Cats*. New York: Crown, 1977.

INTERNET SITES

Because of the changeable nature of the Internet, sites appear and disappear very quickly. These resources offered useful information on cats at the time of publication. Internet addresses must be entered with capital and lowercase letters exactly as they appear.

http://www.yahoo.com
The Yahoo directory of the World Wide Web is an excellent place to find Internet sites on any topic.

Acme Pet
http://www.acmepet.com/

This site provides useful information on cats, including tips on choosing a cat, finding a breeder, grooming, and general care.

American Cat Fanciers Association (ACFA)
P.O. Box 203
Point Lookout, MO 65726
Phone: (417) 334-5430
http://www.acfacat.com/

This organization promotes interest in all domestic, purebred, and nonpurebred cats.

American Society for the Prevention of Cruelty to Animals (ASPCA)
424 East 92nd Street
New York, NY 10128-6804
(212) 876-7700, ext. 4421
http://www.aspca.org/

This organization is dedicated to promoting the welfare and prevention of cruelty to animals. It also provides advice and services for caring for all kinds of animals.

Cat Fanciers' Association
1805 Atlantic Avenue
P.O. Box 1005
Manasquan, NJ 08736-0805
(908) 528-9797
http://www.cfainc.org/cfa/

The world's largest registry of pedigreed cats. The Web site includes information on cat shows, cat breeds, and cat care.

Cat Fanciers' Web Site
http://www.fanciers.com/

This site provides general information about cats and cat care, and includes breed descriptions.

rec.pets.cats FAQ Homepage
http://www.zmall.com/pet/cat-faqs/

This Web site includes lists of questions and answers about cats and cat care.

INDEX

Page numbers in *italics* indicate illustrations.

ABOUT THE AUTHOR

JOHN ZEAMAN is a journalist. For the past thirteen years, he has been a critic, feature writer, and editor with the *Bergen Record* of New Jersey. His interest in pets and animal domestication stems from the numerous pets that have lived in his household, including a standard poodle, two cats, gerbils, a parakeet, finches, lizards, turtles, a garter snake, and, briefly, a wild squirrel. The idea for this series grew out of a project that his daughter did in the fifth grade on the origins of pets. He lives in Leonia, New Jersey, with his wife, Janet, and their children, Claire and Alex.